Date Him

or

Dump Him?

Library of Congress Cataloging in Publication Number: 2004114531

ISBN: 1-59474-038-0

Printed in Singapore
Typeset in Chalet Comprime, Filasophia, and ITC Franklin Gothic Condensed

Designed by Andrea Stephany
Illustrated by Austin Saylor www.sprdlx.com
Edited by Erin Slonaker

Distributed in North America by Chronicle Books
85 Second Street
San Francisco, CA 94105

10 9 8 7 6 5 4 3 2 1

Quirk Books
215 Church Street
Philadelphia, PA 19106
www.quirkbooks.com

Date Him

or

Dump Him?

The No-Nonsense Relationship Quiz

By Melissa Heckscher · Foreword by Anthony Termine, M.D.

QUIRK BOOKS

PHILADELPHIA

Foreword

Romance doesn't have to be complicated.

But, strangely, it oftentimes gets that way. As a psychiatrist working in New York City's trendy SoHo neighborhood, I see it way too much: "He likes me, but . . ." "He's married, but . . ." "He doesn't treat me well, but . . ." In Manhattan, sometimes even not dating gets complicated. The comments I hear are usually along the lines of, "It's so hard to meet someone" or "Everyone always seems so busy."

Really, though, it's simple: You meet someone; you decide if you like him. (Note: The question should always be "Do I like him," not "Does he like me?") But it doesn't usually work that way. Women cling to the wrong guys all the time; men brush off the right girls all the time. Dating has become a game with no concrete set of rules. But there are a set of user-friendly principles that can be applied to dating and relationships. They are as follows:

Don't be afraid of change. Life can be quite difficult at times, and often we are forced to either adapt and change or stay trapped. Have you ever noticed how many people choose to stay trapped? Make a conscious choice to end this cycle.

Take it slow. Whatever happened to foreplay? To meeting someone and having an extraordinary conversation, hoping that it would last? To becoming giddy with anticipation? Most people, in my opinion, move way too fast. A date becomes a relationship before its time, before individuals have time to be themselves and let others see them for who they truly are. Dating should be a long, hopefully pleasurable, interview for the job of "partner," and it takes a lot of questions and answers to fully understand what the job entails. Take the time to find out everything before settling on anyone. Ask a lot of questions. Be candid. There's no need to rush to the "comfortable" stages of a relationship. Enjoy the beginning; it can be exhilarating.

Have fun. If you're in a relationship and you're not having fun together, you probably should not be a couple.

Don't pretend. A common mistake many women make is acting how they think a man wants them to act. Bad move. All that pretending eventually becomes tiring, and then the real person comes out. If you want someone to like you, he has to like you, not the person you're pretending to be. I say if you want to act, do it on stage. If you try to present yourself as perfect and always agreeable, you're just creating a fantasy.

Don't be afraid to disagree. Roadblocks along the way are common. Watch out for comments such as, "We never argue." You should argue sometimes, at least a little bit. Recognize that roadblocks are useful; they provide a "time out" during which we can collect our thoughts and refuel. Try to work through these obstacles and understand the significance of the event itself. While every event doesn't have to be a disaster, it shouldn't be ignored either. What defines a healthy relationship is how the two of you work through your inherent differences.

Work on yourself. Relationships require work. A loving relationship can be fulfilling, but if it becomes all-consuming it can be toxic. Don't be defined by your relationship. Retain your individuality, continue to work on your goals, and make time for yourself outside the relationship. This allows a healthy perspective to flourish, and it makes for more interesting conversation. The best thing about relationships is that they give us the opportunity to learn about ourselves. They help us grow, mature, and evolve into more interesting individuals. When one person stops contributing, things can get really dull.

Finally, one last word of advice: **Don't take it all so seriously.** Things change. Let your life be a journey. Welcome new experiences, and try not to have expectations. Don't be defined by old-fashioned ideals: People can have more than one "true love." Keep all of this in mind as you assess the status of your current relationship in the following pages. Remember: All relationships are different—we are the ones that change, hopefully for the better. The full package—love, lust, trust, companionship, responsibility—is attainable, and it does exist.

Anthony Termine, M.D.
New York, New York

Introduction

Date Him or Dump Him? is the product of a breakup. Or, to be fair, a series of breakups.

The latest guy's story? He hadn't gotten over his ex-girlfriend. The guy before him was too young. The one before that, too weird. Somewhere along the way there's been a too far away, a too arrogant, a too boring, a too good a friend, and a too busy. In my years of dating, I've managed to get a lot of "too-somethings" and too much time spent worrying about them.

It got me thinking: What if I could come up with a formula that would determine the outcome of a relationship before it started? A test that could tell if it's going to work before you wasted too much time trying?

Most often it's clear within the first few dates whether you're headed toward relationship territory. Maybe he only calls you once a week, maybe he spends too much time at the office, maybe he lives hours away. Maybe, if you're lucky, he calls you all the time, he can't stop telling you how great you look, and he sometimes introduces you as his girlfriend.

It's not rocket science, but women often pretend it is. They make excuses (He's really busy at work these days), they justify his not calling (Maybe he lost his cell phone?), they pick apart his most simple behaviors and make them complicated (Maybe he was too nervous to talk to me?). But like anything else, the most obvious explanation is usually the right one.

The "formula" that creates the structure of this book was based on a combination of personal experiences, interviews, and informal questionnaires on the subject of dating and relationships. Keep in mind that every relationship has its quirks, and no book could account for all of them. In general, though, the way he treats you in the beginning is generally the way he'll treat you later. By taking a close look at how he's treating you now, this quiz can determine what the relationship will be like later.

If the result of the quiz tells you you're bound for love, lust, and commitment, enjoy it! If not, don't be afraid to end things. After all, ending one thing always starts something else, and whatever comes next might be exactly what you're looking for.

So don't overanalyze. Don't let yourself get stepped on. And, most important, don't stay with one of those "too-something" guys—there are better guys out there.

Have fun, and happy dating!

How to Use this Book

This book is designed to predict the outcome of a new relationship. It works best when used within the first few weeks to the first few months of seeing a new guy, when you're not completely new to each other but you haven't yet established "what's going on."

This book is not meant to be read cover to cover. Turn only to the pages directed by your choices. And be honest. Manipulating your answers to achieve a desired outcome defeats the purpose. It's always best to go with your first instincts; they're always the most truthful.

Disclaimer: This book is meant to be used for entertainment purposes only. Should it result in heartbreak, disappointment, confusion, anger, or any other conditions related to love, unrequited or otherwise, the author and publisher are not liable.

This book can be used as many times as you have relationships. Good luck!

Turn to page 2.

Timing

Timing is one of the most critical (perhaps *the* most critical) things that can make or break a relationship. If he just broke up with his longtime girlfriend, chances are he's not all that eager to jump into another relationship. But you never know—he could be one of those serial monogamists, for whom being single doesn't last long.

There is one thing to be said for a guy who was in a long-term relationship, though: He was *in* a *long-term relationship*! And that means he's got an attention span longer than a first grader's, he's got something you might find worth sticking around for, and he may want a relationship again . . .

When was he last in a serious relationship?

Within the past three months. *Turn to page 3.*
Between three months and one year ago. *Turn to page 5.*
More than a year ago. *Turn to page 7.*
He's never been in a serious relationship. *Turn to page 9.*
He's still in a relationship (with someone else). *Turn to page 10.*
I'm not sure. We haven't talked about it. *Turn to page 199.*

Proceed with Caution

Look, this guy *just* got out of a relationship. No matter what crazy chemistry the two of you might be feeling, he's probably not all that eager to jump back into the land of Saturday-night movie rentals and "Did you just look at another girl?" showdowns.

But who knows. Maybe you're his magic, special someone. Maybe he's already forgotten all about that pesky ex (sadly, unlikely). Don't worry: It's not you. You could be a Lakers cheerleader with a genius IQ and a great sense of humor, and you *still* wouldn't be likely to snag a freshly released boyfriend.

You really think you might have a chance? You'd better pay close attention to the signs. Like, how often does he call?

Turn to page 4.

"I'll be in touch"

Even if he's a player who's had more girlfriends than late-night slices of pizza, any guy who's interested in a girl will call or e-mail her at least once every few days.

And you can forget the "rules" of dating. Most guys who really like a girl aren't going to follow the so-called Three-Day Rule, which says a guy should postpone calling for at least 72 hours.

How often do you hear from him (by e-mail or phone)?

Every day. *Turn to page 11.*
Every few days. *Turn to page 13.*
Once a week or less. *Turn to page 15.*

Almost a Rebound

OK, so you're not exactly a rebound. You're not the long-awaited glass of water at the end of the Mojave Desert, either. Depending on how much his last girl-friend meant to him—and how much she's trying to get him back—your guy may still be in her clutches.

Turn to page 6.

Kicked to the Curb

In relationships, the person who cuts the ties is generally the person who's OK moving on. If your guy was the dumpee, he may still be too deep in the pool of rejection to crawl out and find someone new. (This doesn't mean he's too bruised to date; rather, he just might not be ready to get serious.) If he was the dumper, he may be ready—perhaps even eager—to find a replacement.

Who ended his last relationship?

She did. *Turn to page 17.*
He did. *Turn to page 19.*
It was mutual. *Turn to page 20.*

Ready for Action

Congratulations. You've snagged a single guy who's probably not so mired down in the aftermath of a breakup that he can't see a girl as something more than just a living "Warning: Do Not Cross" line.

But just because he falls into the ready-to-date category doesn't mean he's ready to date *you*. This guy's had a while to marinate in his bachelordom; he may actually like it there. Honestly, though, that's a good thing: You want a guy who's comfortable being alone, and those nights you spend cuddling on the couch watching movies with your guy will mean all the more knowing he gave up his bachelor days for you.

So things seem promising. But there's more to a relationship than just finding an available guy.

Turn to page 8.

The Art of Conversation

You and he don't have to share the same taste in movies, have the same CD in your car stereo, and both want to spend every Sunday camped out in front of the TV watching sports. But you should be able to talk about why you don't like his favorite CD, why you hated that movie, and why you'd rather spend an afternoon on a hike than in front of the tube.

Getting a relationship to work isn't as much about having everything in common as it is about how you work with what you *don't* have in common and how you work as a couple. In other words: Can you carry on a meaningful conversation?

How much do you have to talk about?

Not much. *Turn to page 115.*
Anything and everything. *Turn to page 22.*
We don't really talk at all; we're too busy making out. *Turn to page 25.*

The Bachelor

Wait, this guy's *never* had a girlfriend? Not ever?

Assuming that he's not in middle school (or the seminary), you've got to ask yourself the very important question: "Why not?"

By the time we're in our 20s, most of us have tested the dating waters more than once. Those who haven't even dipped a toe in may be wrestling with some commitment issues. Maybe this guy just hasn't found "the one" yet, in which case he may have too-high standards. His age will give you some idea of how long he's been on the dating scene.

How old is he?

Under 20. *Turn to page 23.*
21 to 25. *Turn to page 27.*
26 to 30. *Turn to page 59.*
31 or older. *Turn to page 30.*

Is he married?

Yes. *Turn to page 31.*
No, but he has a girlfriend. *Turn to page 73.*

Frequency

So he's making the calls. That's certainly comforting. But of course, face-to-face time is what really makes a relationship happen. Are you seeing him a lot, too?

Turn to page 12.

How often do you see him?

Nearly every day. *Turn to page 32.*
Every few days. *Turn to page 68.*
Once a week. *Turn to page 194.*
Once a month (or less). *Turn to page 29.*

Boyfriend Mode

Wow, he just got out of a relationship and he *still* calls you on a fairly regular basis. Things are looking good.

But you never know. Maybe he's just lonely. Maybe he's so used to having a girlfriend that he just likes having *somebody* around. So you'd better do a little sleuthing: How did it end with his ex? If he's the one who ended things, you're more likely to have an emotionally available boyfriend. If she ended it, he may just be missing having someone—*anyone*—around.

Turn to page 6.

Taking the Lead

Guys are usually pretty easy to ask out, despite what you might think. With no other conflicts, a man is likely to accept your invitation. He may not want to go to Sunday dinner at your parents' place, but the movies on Tuesday? Sure thing.

Still, if you get the feeling that he's going out with you just because you happened to catch him at a good time and he had nothing better to do, you may be dating a guy who's not really dating you.

Like it or not, guys are generally raised with the expectation that they will pursue women they're interested in. If you're doing all the pursuing, you may want to slow it down a bit and see if he'll take the lead.

Turn to page 18.

Playing the Field?

It's most likely that he's not calling you very often because, to put it bluntly, he doesn't want to call you very often.

Calling a girl on a regular basis means starting something—whether that be a short-lived fling or a three-and-a-half year relationship that leads to marriage. Maybe neither scenario appeals to him right now.

He seems content to make the least amount of effort necessary to keep you waiting by the phone. If he can skirt by with minimal effort while maintaining a hassle-free (once every so often) "relationship" with you, he'll do it for as long as he can.

Turn to page 139.

Exceeding Daily Dosage?

Ahhh, love. You meet. You flirt. You feel those magical sparks of attraction. Then you toss out all the pieces that made you an individual to create a new you; namely, a "you" that really means "us." Romantic, isn't it?

It might feel good to know this guy wants to see you all the time. And maybe you want to see him all the time, too. But do you really want your life to become one in which every sentence begins with "We" instead of "I"?

If you and the girls felt like catching a movie without him tagging along, would it be a problem? Would he be upset if you spent Saturday relaxing—alone—in the park instead of hanging with him? **Does he get upset when you do things without him?**

Yes, he wants me to be with him all the time. *Turn to page 57.*
No, he's okay with spending time apart. *Turn to page 35.*

Pain of Rejection

Uh-oh. She ended things. This is a potential bad sign. Most guys hate rejection, and it only makes the relationship seem more important than it was in the first place. (Women do it, too: "Wait, he didn't want me? Now I want him more!") So watch yourself with this one—he may be too busy wondering if she's moved on to care whether you like the way he looks in that tie.

But maybe he's more mature and has moved on. In any case, he's probably already showing you—without trying—exactly how he feels. Men aren't too hard to read; it's just small print—you need to look closely.

Turn to page 14.

Who initiates most of your dates?

He does. *Turn to page 119.*
I do. *Turn to page 33.*

The Ex Factor

OK, he ended things. That's a potentially good sign. But sometimes guys end relationships because relationships are going to end anyway—he knew it was coming and just made the first move. If that's the case, he may have been acting just to spare himself the pain of rejection.

You've got to figure out how much The Ex still means to him. If he thinks about her all the time, working her into conversation, he's probably too attached to the idea of her to move on to the idea—and reality—of you.

Does her picture still sit on his bedside table? Does he still talk about her every time he wears that green sweater she gave him three years ago? **Is his ex still a part of his life?**

No. All her stuff is gone, and he doesn't talk about her (unless I ask).
Turn to page 35.

Yes. They're friends now, but I don't think there's anything going on.
Turn to page 37.

Yes. He still talks about her, and she keeps calling him to try to "make up."
Turn to page 36.

Mutual Schmutual

"It was mutual." If it has to end, this is what we all hope for. We picture two level-headed, self-respecting people trying to make a relationship work but gently and happily parting ways when it doesn't.

The truth: It almost never happens that way, and unfortunately, it doesn't mean he's exempt from broken-hearted rants and strong late-night urges to call her and ask if she's seeing someone new. A mutual breakup is still a breakup; it's simply one that happened under the guise of agreement.

Turn to page 105.

Are you attracted to him?

Definitely! *Turn to page 40.*
Not really. *Turn to page 45.*

Common Ground

You've got things to talk about. Are you attracted to each other, too? After all, that's really the only thing separating friendship from romance.

Are you attracted to him?

Yes. *Turn to page 128.*
Sometimes. *Turn to page 69.*
Not really. *Turn to page 39.*

Baby Talk

OK, there's a reason why he's never had a long-term girlfriend: He's never had a long-term anything.

Generally, teenagers aren't ready for commitments that last long past graduation. But it's not like it never happens. Lots of happy couples were once high-school sweethearts.

Turn to page 8.

Something to Smile About

A relationship without laughter is like popcorn without butter. It might be OK, but who wants just OK? Science has proven laughter to be more beneficial to your health than even, say, sex. So ask yourself:

Do you make each other laugh?

Yes. *Turn to page 67.*
Nope, but the passion makes up for it.
Turn to page 52.

Skin Deep

In the beginning, a relationship can coast by on physical terms alone without either side asking anything more profound than "Your place or mine?" After all, why complicate matters with the whole words-and-sentences thing?

But let's be real. After the thrill of doing nothing more than making out wears off, it's only a matter of time before one of you begins to wonder, "What else is there?"

Turn to page 24.

Part of His Life

A guy who really wants to get closer to a woman will do what he can to include her in his life. We're talking everything from meeting his friends and seeing where he works to disclosing which side of the bed is "his side" and exactly how many shots of espresso he likes in his morning mocha java.

If he hasn't given you full disclosure yet (or even partial disclosure), he may not be ready to let you in.

How much does he include you in his life?

He tells me everything about his job, his friends, and his family, and I've already met most of the people he's close to. *Turn to page 72.*

He's pretty busy. I've met a few of his friends, and he tries to include me when he can. *Turn to page 144.*

When we hang out, it's just the two of us. *Turn to page 125.*

Happily Single

So maybe he didn't meet the girl of his dreams in college, or maybe he's just pickier than most guys. He's still young, and girlfriends aren't a prerequisite for growing up. In fact, it might be a good thing that he's remained free for so long. By now, he probably knows what he wants, and he doesn't have a bad breakup lurking in his past to keep him from moving forward.

So let's get on to the more important questions.

Turn to page 34.

In the Eye(s) of the Beholder

We hate to perpetuate the cult of beauty, but let's face it: Looks matter—at least a little bit. And while it's true most women will happily choose sincerity and confidence over a chiseled jaw and six-pack abs, there's something to be said for finding our mates pleasant to look at.

If your guy's a ringer for an underwear model with a perfect complexion and an unbearably gorgeous smile, there's a chance he's single because . . . he wants to be. Period. Too many choices sometimes leads to not making choices at all. ("Why choose this one when there's that one . . . and that one . . . and that one?")

Is he cute?

Definitely! He looks like a model. *Turn to page 58.*
Nah, he's nothing extraordinary. *Turn to page 158.*

Mileage Matters

Generally, seeing a guy once a month signifies a problem. The only acceptable reason for such infrequency is if you're doing the long-distance thing.

Where does he live?

In the neighborhood. Turn to page 115.
A few hours' drive. Turn to page 71.
It takes a plane ride. Turn to page 43.

The Confirmed Bachelor

Assuming this guy isn't crazy, in prison, or growing grotesque wads of hair from both nostrils, he should have had at least *some* chance in his fifteen years or so of post-pubescence to find himself a girlfriend.

There are a few things that might be happening here: (1) He's holding out for the "right" girl; (2) no girl can stand him long enough to attain relationship status; (3) he just prefers being single; or (4) he's a priest.

If it's number 4, there's not much you can do—at least, nothing that won't condemn him to a fiery afterlife. So let's look at some of the other options:

Has he had many short-term relationships (including one-night stands)?

Yes. *Turn to page 38.*
No. *Turn to page 146.*

**Is he still living with his wife,
or are they separated?**

Living with her. *Turn to page 155.*
They're separated. *Turn to page 49.*

Do you live together?

Yes. *Turn to page 50.*
No. *Turn to page 56.*

The Available Guy

He might not be banging down your door, but it appears, at the very least, he's available when you want to bang down his. But what kind of "available" is that? There's the physically available (all too common), the platonically available (not so common), and the emotionally available (almost unheard of). Which type of guy are you dealing with?

What do you spend your time doing?

I'd say our relationship is mostly physical. *Turn to page 52.*

Watching TV, going to the movies—doing other things that don't involve much conversation. *Turn to page 53.*

Anything and everything: We can be silly together, we can talk until the sun comes up, and we can sit together in silence (comfortably). *Turn to page 153.*

How much time does he spend with you?

A lot. We see each other almost every day. *Turn to page 57.*

A fair amount—we hang out at least once a week. *Turn to page 114.*

Not much. I'm lucky if I see him two or three times a month.
Turn to page 188.

QUIZ RESULT: You Beat the Odds!

Advice: Enjoy it! But be careful.

You had everything stacked against you, yet it appears you've won. Sure, you were the rebound to his rocky romantic past, but whatever you've got, it's working! Your guy may just be one of those people who can go through a breakup and come out the better for it.

But be a little cautious. There's something a little worrisome about a guy who can find a new "love" so quickly. It's like this: He's either got the romantic equivalent of ADD, or you're just It for him.

Let's hope it's the latter. If not, let's hope he's on Ritalin.

Plagued by the Past

Even if he's screening his calls, has changed his locks, and insists he's moved on, a guy who's still getting calls from a whining ex-girlfriend is not going to have an easy ride toward new horizons (that being you).

Most men would rather sit through back-to-back screenings of *Beaches* than endure the cries and shameless "Can't-we-get-back-together" pleas of a weepy ex. Just because he doesn't want her back doesn't mean it'll be smooth sailing for him and you. The torture of a clingy ex just might make him long for the joys of single life.

Does he seem upset or bothered when he talks about his ex-girlfriend?

Yes. *Turn to page 70.*
No. *Turn to page 26.*

Staying Friends

A guy who can stay on good terms with an ex-girlfriend is a guy who is mature enough to navigate a breakup without losing his cool—or losing sight of what he still likes about his ex.

If he was a total jerk to his ex, chances are she wouldn't want to stick around for the occasional lunch or the every-so-often "So, how have you been?" telephone conversation. Breakup-born friendships take effort, strength, and maturity.

On the flip side, the emotional baggage of a breakup is a heavy load to toss out, and it's a safe bet that he still has some feelings for his newly made "friend." Like a recovering alcoholic in a wine bar, a guy spending *too* much time with an ex-girlfriend could lead to a regression.

Turn to page 107.

Thinking About the Future

By the time they're in their 30s, most guys tend to at least think about marriage. They may not want it to happen next week. Or even next year. But a funny thing happens when guys start seeing their friends walk down that aisle: They start to ask themselves, "Am I a bachelor or a bridegroom?"

Does he ever talk about wanting to settle down eventually?

No. *Turn to page 44.*
Yes. *Turn to page 7.*

QUIZ RESULT: Just Friends

Advice: Friendship is where it's at.

This is an all-too-common scenario. One person feels something; the other, nothing. And there's not a whole lot you can do about it.

At some point, one of you might have considered testing the waters—maybe gulping a few shots of tequila, closing your eyes, and attempting a kiss just to see what it feels like.

The truth: It probably won't be so bad. But it certainly won't be fantastic. Attraction isn't a guessing game. If you don't feel it now, you're not going to feel it then, either.

But don't worry. You seem to get along well (as friends), so if you can both deal with the platonic vibe, why not try something a bit less hormonally charged than making out? Ping-Pong, anyone?

Is he attracted to you?

He seems to be! He's always telling me how great I look, and sometimes I catch him watching me from across the room. *Turn to page 99.*

I'm not sure. He seldom comments on my appearance, and he doesn't really look at me "that way." *Turn to page 39.*

That "Something Special"

It's clear he's into you. But are you into him? When the two of you spend the night "watching TV on the couch," does any actual TV get watched? In other words: **How's the chemistry?**

Good, we're all over each other. *Turn to page 117.*
We're more friends than lovers. *Turn to page 55.*

Potential for Overload

Dating a coworker or a classmate can be fun, but it's also got the potential for major overload. Just think: You're already seeing him *almost* all the time; now you're going to see him *all* the time. Being this attached to a person is only beneficial if it involves an umbilical cord and a womb.

How often do you see him outside of school or work?

Every day. *Turn to page 57.*

Every few days. *Turn to page 68.*

Every few weeks (or less). *Turn to page 165.*

QUIZ RESULT: Long-Distance Lovers

Advice: Move, or move on.

"Absence makes the heart grow fonder," they say. But it also makes the heart grow lonely, worried, jealous, and sad.

Long-distance relationships aren't as wonderful as those steamy romance novels make them out to be. Most of the time, they're a recipe for self-doubt and emotional exhaustion.

Sure, they can work. We all know someone who knows someone who had a long-distance relationship that ended in a blissful marriage. But generally, trying to maintain a relationship from afar is sort of like trying to graduate high school when you're skipping school every day; if you haven't been in class, you're probably not going to pass the exam.

It's simple: If it's meant to be, make "it" a little bit closer.

QUIZ RESULT: The Lifelong Bachelor

Advice: Have fun, but don't expect much.

Maybe he prefers one-night stands to lifelong partners. While society likes to vilify those who do not choose the traditional road of love, marriage, and offspring, there's really nothing wrong with them.

If you want someone a little more compatible with your parenting plans, look elsewhere. There are men out there looking to settle down; go find yourself one of them.

However, if short-term fun is your thing, this guy probably knows how to do it. After all, he's *been* doing it. And doing it. So enjoy it, and him, and put off the long-term commitment until you find a guy a little more willing to bottle-feed (and we're not talking beer bottles).

QUIZ RESULT: No Sizzle

Advice: Find someone else.

Let's be honest, it's hard to maintain a romantic relationship when there's no romance. And when you'd rather watch the end of that TV movie of the week than make out with your guy—well, that's certainly not romantic.

Not to say that physical intimacy is the most important part of a relationship; it's not. But it does make things a little more fun when you're tired of playing chess or talking about your day. It also makes the honeymoon a whole lot more exciting.

Don't worry though. Just because *he* didn't work out doesn't mean that someone else won't.

So Far So Good

Things look good so far. You've got stuff to talk about; you're attracted to each other. But is he ready?

Guys are strange creatures and often deathly afraid of that word that begins with "r" and ends with "elationship." It's hard to understand the guy who will stop at nothing to maintain his independence, even if it means shrugging off that well-adjusted, pretty, smart woman he's dating to keep himself free and clear of any attachments.

You need to assess just how much he thinks about you.

Turn to page 64.

QUIZ RESULT: The Scarlet Letter

Advice: Get out while you can.

For those of you who flunked ninth-grade English, the scarlet letter of *The Scarlet Letter* is an "A" for adultery. As in, what you're doing.

A woman can find plenty of reasons to justify dating a married man. Maybe she doesn't want a commitment. Maybe it's the thrill of secrecy. Or maybe—as is most often the case—the guy is telling her his marriage isn't going well and that he's going to get out of it but that "it just takes time." Well, you know what? That might be true. But any *real* man is going to get out of it *before* messing around with someone else.

Do yourself, his wife, and all the other people the inevitable divorce will involve (e.g., children, family members, friends, therapists, lawyers, and IRS agents) a favor and dump the guy.

QUIZ RESULT: Religious Differences

Advice: Save yourself for someone else.

If you don't mind a nonsexual relationship without the possibility of a long-term commitment, you might be able to squeeze out a good few months with this guy. But don't expect much more than that.

Think about it: If religious disparities can divide nations throughout history, it can surely put a rift in your romantic endeavors. He's not likely to see it your way, and you're not likely to drop everything and be reborn . . . are you?

You have two options: Give up whatever spiritual or religious identity you have now and convert to his religion (this only works if you wholeheartedly support it—and truly think he's The One), or find a guy whose faith doesn't get in the way of your affections.

'Til Death Do Us . . . Oops.

Being separated isn't a fun, happy place for most guys. Usually, they're caught somewhere between wanting to take advantage of their freedom and wanting to nestle back into the safety of a relationship.

A guy in this position may be really into you for now, but at any moment he may retreat, with the frantic exclamation of "Slow down!" or "I need space!" or "Maybe I won't sign those divorce papers after all!"

In other words, watch your step. Some guys will go years before feeling comfortable starting something new; others will dive in head first. Of course, those that jump in without testing how deep the water is may hit the bottom.

Turn to page 156.

Speed Demons

You obviously picked up the wrong book. What you *meant* to grab was *How to Mess Up a New Relationship by Moving at WARP SPEED*. This book is for people who just started dating, not for people who just started sharing a bathtub and a gas bill.

Were you roommates before you started dating this guy?

No. *Turn to page 51.*
Yes. *Turn to page 83.*

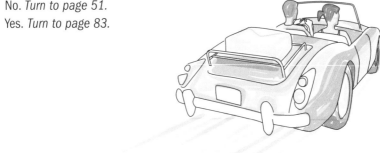

QUIZ RESULT: Fast-Track Love

Advice: Like you're going to listen.

Falling in love at top speed is a little like getting a really trendy haircut at a pricey salon. At first, it's great—the cucumber slices on the eyes, the scalp massage, the stylists gathered around you. But then you wake up the next day and see that "layered bob" falling around your ears like an out-of-control mullet, and it hits you: You made an impulsive, expensive mistake.

In relationships, that pricey mistake is moving way too fast. In the beginning, spending every waking moment with your guy, maybe even moving in together, is romantic. Passionate. And then somewhere down the line, you find yourself thinking: "I used to have a life!" It's best to wait until you really know a guy before shacking up with him. That way, there's less risk of any big surprises once you're sharing the bills.

QUIZ RESULT: Base Attraction

Advice: Enjoy it if you want it.

If it's a physical relationship you're looking for, you've got it. Nothing wrong with that. But if you want a little more than a roll in the hay, you may want to look elsewhere.

This guy isn't ready to give up his freedom just yet. Even though he likes being around you, it doesn't look like he's ready to be your boyfriend. It's okay to have fun with a guy without expecting to marry him. And as long as you're not waiting around for love, flowers, or someone who provides stimulating conversation, you've got nothing to lose by letting the sparks fly.

Bottom line: If you're just looking for a good time, this is your guy. After all, he's up for anything. Well, except anything serious.

QUIZ RESULT: Just Passing Through

Advice: Don't get too attached.

You've caught yourself a guy who's not ready to be caught. And since he's not putting in much effort, you probably won't have him for long.

But you have him now. And really, you have most of the ingredients of a relationship—friendship, attraction, comfort. You can't blame him for not being ready for anything serious. In the same way a dog learns to associate crossing an electric fence with "STOP!" your guy has probably had some "training" that has led him to rank intimacy right up there with electric shock therapy.

And as long as you don't sit around stressing over why he doesn't do more with you, everything will be just fine. And you never know: Someday he may get over his "girlfriend phobia" and see you in a whole new light.

Either that, or you'll get tired of the invisible fence and find a guy who's ready to tear off the collar and get out of the yard altogether.

Talk of the Future

Things are looking pretty good between you two. But what about your future? Guys who don't mind making plans with you, whether it's a movie this weekend or a trip to Mexico next April, are essentially saying that they expect you to stick around.

Does he make plans with you ahead of time?

Yes, we plan everything from movie dates a few days from now to romantic getaways that are months off. *Turn to page 41.*

We never commit to things more than a few days ahead of time.
Turn to page 53.

QUIZ RESULT: Friends with Benefits

Advice: Figure out how you're benefiting.

You may be going through the superficial motions of a relationship, but a few movie dates and the occasional breakfast do not a relationship make. What you've got with this guy is more of a friendship than a "boyfriendship." Sure, you may be attracted to each other. But relationships are like puzzles—you need to have *all* the pieces to make them come together.

You know as well as he does that there's something missing in your collective time together. It could be as simple as . . . love? Or as complicated as, well . . . love?

It's also possible that one of you is still reeling from a past relationship. If that's the case, let him go. Sometimes it's necessary for a person to soak up all the sadness, to really understand it, before moving on.

Do you work or go to school together?

Yes. *Turn to page 42.*
No. *Turn to page 16.*

QUIZ RESULT: Too Much of a Good Thing

Advice: Slow down.

It doesn't take a genius to figure this one out: He likes you. A lot. Maybe too much. And, sure, everything seems just peachy and happy and perfect, and, like, "Isn't he the *best*?"

Well . . . no. There's a wonderful thing that exists between people, without which we'd most definitely all drive each other crazy. It's called space; you might want to give it a try.

You *did* just start dating him, and normally, a relationship that kicks into high gear before it gets a chance to warm up is destined for a breakdown.

Here's some advice for both of you: Take a deep breath. Count to 10. Now go into separate corners. See what happens. Then tell each other all about it tomorrow.

"I'm Too Sexy"

Let's take a moment to ponder why Mr. Perfect has never had a girlfriend. Could it be that there's not much more to him than his muscular abs and perfect skin? Or maybe with all that sexiness under his belt, he feels like "life is too short" to tie himself down to just one girl—or even remember her name!

Historically speaking, great-looking guys aren't the ones scrounging around desperately for a girlfriend. Perhaps there's something lurking beneath his sparkling exterior that's not so beautiful? Let's start with the obvious:

Does he seem arrogant?

Yes. *Turn to page 60.*
No. *Turn to page 62.*

The Late Bloomer

When a guy wants to move from "just dating" to being in a relationship, it's generally as simple as asking the girl he's with if she wants to get serious. Easy.

Now consider the fact that your guy has gone through puberty, high school, and at least a good two, three years as a bona fide grown-up without finding at least one girl he wanted to commit to. He's either got issues with intimacy or he just prefers playing the field.

Turn to page 28.

The Narciss-Single

They say you can never love anyone until you love yourself. But they never said what happens when you love yourself too much. The most likely scenario? All that loving leaves no room for anyone else.

What you've got is a guy who probably rarely makes real connections, because real connections would require him to actually care about someone other than himself and to have a little bit of humility—which he doesn't have.

But hey, at least he looks good. That counts for a lot, right? Wrong. Grandma always said, "Never go out with a man who's better looking than you are." Why? Well, according to dear old Grams, being the prettier of the pair ensures that you'll be put on a pedestal. And it's nice to be worshipped, or at least appreciated, by your guy.

Does he make you feel good about yourself?

Yes, he's always complimenting me. *Turn to page 53.*

No, he doesn't make any effort to show me that he thinks I'm even half as attractive as he thinks he is! *Turn to page 61.*

QUIZ RESULT: The Stuck-Up Jerk

Advice: Save your energy for someone who appreciates you.

Here's a tip: Getting the best-looking guy around—unless he's as nice as he is hot—is not an instant upper for your self-esteem. In fact, it'll probably leave you feeling worse than before, because this type of self-centered guy is often more into building stronger abs than stronger relationships.

You'll always have bragging rights—the nonchalant, "Yeah, I used to date him." But if anyone sticks around to hear the rest of the story, it'll inevitably end with something like "He was a total jerk," "He was so vain," or "He dumped me for a Norwegian volleyball player; you can see her in this month's issue of *Maxim*."

A boyfriend should be just one bright spot in your life, not the defining aspect of it. Eventually, you've got to realize that no guy can make you feel fulfilled. Only you can do that.

Chronic Single-Guy Syndrome?

Assuming he's not a sociopath and he didn't spend Life Until You locked in an institution, he's no doubt had prior opportunities to find someone to love. But for whatever reason, it appears he's chosen to opt out. Perhaps he just enjoys being single. If this is the case, he'd be showing some definite Chronic Single-Guy attributes, such as a jam-packed weekend social schedule and a constantly ringing cell phone.

When you go out with him, does his cell phone seem to be ringing all the time?

Yeah, it rings a lot. *Turn to page 63.*
No, it doesn't ring much. *Turn to page 8.*
He doesn't have a cell phone. *Turn to page 79.*

Hello?

Phone etiquette is a simple thing. When you're out with someone you respect—and this goes for everyone from business associates to first dates—you turn your ringer off or ignore the call (unless you're a heart surgeon or a man awaiting the any-minute-now birth of his first child—and if your guy falls into the latter category, it's unlikely he's going to be on a date with you anyhow).

If this man is letting his phone ring throughout your date or keeps jumping to answer it every time it vibrates, he's severely lacking in manners. And this can only mean one of two things: (1) His mom didn't bring him up right, or (2) he's not trying to impress you.

Does he answer the calls?

Yes, and he usually spends a few minutes (or more) talking on the phone. *Turn to page 65.*
Yeah, but he only stays on for a few seconds. *Turn to page 182.*
No, he lets voicemail pick up unless he's expecting a really important call. *Turn to page 64.*

A Little Extra

If he's stopping by your place unexpectedly just because he's "in the neighborhood"; if he's brewing a pot of chicken noodle soup the moment you tell him you're not feeling well; if he's so into your dates that he doesn't even remember he *has* a cell phone, let alone answer it, it'd be safe to say that he likes you.

Does he go out of his way for you?

Yes. *Turn to page 91.*
No. *Turn to page 80.*

Who's Calling?

Unless he's a doctor, an undercover agent of some sort, or a volunteer for a suicide hotline, there's really no good reason he has to be on the phone when he's out with you. They made voicemail for a reason.

The fact that he can't refuse the beck and call of his phone means he'd rather ignore you than that catchy little ring tone.

Turn to page 66.

QUIZ RESULT: ADD Guy

Advice: Break out the Ritalin.

It looks like your guy's got the attention span of a Jack Russell terrier. You know the type—you think he's focused on you and all ready to "stay," but next thing you know, he's halfway down the block chasing the mailman. Or mailwoman.

Life is full of distractions. Most people know how to deal with them, and it's usually as simple as activating the "Ringer Off" function or turning off the television when they're in the middle of an important conversation.

This guy either doesn't know how to show you some basic consideration or he doesn't care to. In either case, he's not worth it—he hardly seems interested in making you a part of his life. Unless you don't mind sharing his attention with other women, his voicemail, or a truckload of distractions, your best bet is to excuse yourself from the relationship (if you want to call it that) for good. You can explain it all to him later. Just leave a message.

QUIZ RESULT: Temporary Happiness

Advice: It works for now.

Every now and then, when we're fed up with looking for the Right One, we find ourselves settling for the Wrong One who can take our thoughts off the search for a while.

Unfortunately, the Wrong One is, well, wrong. So it doesn't usually last.

You two aren't perfect for each other. But you're not terrible for each other, either. If you look deep within, you both know it's not true love, but not everything needs to be perfect. Sometimes, all we want is someone to play the part for a little while.

So enjoy the role-playing and be sure not to get so swept up in the show that you forget what you were looking for in the first place.

Just remember: You can't make a Wrong a Right. Don't try.

Time Together

Seeing someone every few days is the perfect amount of time to say "I like you" without saying "I like you so much, I'm going to extinguish the rest of my life and suffocate you with my constant presence." Every few days is good. It enables you to maintain your own life rather than let it slip away and become someone else's.

Turn to page 99.

Turn to page 99.

68

QUIZ RESULT: The "Sometimes" Lover

Advice: "Sometimes" usually means "never."

You like spending time with your guy, but you seldom feel the sparks—unless you've had a few vodka tonics. Look, the attraction's either there or it's not.

Think about it: How often do you hear Grandpa waxing nostalgic about the night he met Grandma, saying, "I was really hammered, and for those three hours, she was the most beautiful woman I'd ever seen"? Most likely, never. And that's because "sometimes" attractions generally fizzle out in about the same amount of time it takes the tonic in your drink to go flat.

Do yourself a favor and stick to being friends with this guy: You're good at it, and it'll work better that way.

Ex Issues

The opposite of love isn't hate; it's indifference. So the fact that your guy still seems bothered when he talks about his ex probably means she still means something to him.

Generally, when a person is over something, it doesn't faze him to talk about it. And if he can share what he learned from the relationship or tell the very occasional funny anecdote without getting emotional about it, you know it's really over. But if he gets in a funk every time her name comes up, he probably hasn't come to terms with the idea that it's over (even if he says he has).

If he's still stewing about the tribulations of a past relationship, odds are he doesn't have a whole lot of emotional space left for you.

Turn to page 86.

Hours Apart

Sure, right now a few hours' drive to get to his place is no biggie. It's romantic. You'd walk to his place if you had to. But fast-forward six months, when you haven't seen him in three weeks because neither of you feels like spending 60 bucks on gas and driving six hours.

It's this simple: If your guy lives far enough away that you have to make a pit stop on the way to his house, then you may as well consider yourselves long-distance lovers. That means romantic weekends together interspersed with long weeks apart.

Generally, this kind of relationship works only when there's a light at the end of the tunnel or you already have a solid history together.

Turn to page 43.

Do you include him in your life?

Yes, he's already a part of my social circle.
Turn to page 196.

No, I'm not ready to let him in just yet.
Turn to page 142.

He's Taken

Even the best relationships have their share of struggles, but, ideally, they don't show up until later on. Picking a guy who already has a girlfriend packs in problems right from the beginning. This is especially true if his lust for you is taking him away from a live-in girlfriend or someone he's been seeing for several years. It's hard to compete with a history.

How long has he been with his girlfriend (the one he's cheating on)?

More than a year. *Turn to page 75.*
Less than a year. *Turn to page 133.*

Excuses, Excuses

If this were a long-distance thing, maybe that would explain his lack of reciprocity and attentiveness. No luck there; he's just not calling you. And why is that?

Maybe he's not a phone person. Then again, maybe he's just not a phone-you person. Let's give him the benefit of the doubt for now. No matter how good you may look in a bikini and how great your first date was, some guys will always put their careers first. His job could be the reason why you're not hearing from him as much as you'd like.

Turn to page 166.

Are they living together?

Yes. *Turn to page 76.*
No. *Turn to page 140.*

As Good as Married

Living together as a married couple and living together as a nonmarried couple are pretty much the same thing minus the wedding ring and the pestering in-laws.

The peripherals might be different. For instance, you don't need a lawyer should you decide it's not working out. But the hard wiring's the same: You wake up together. You fall asleep together. You debate the phone bill charges together. Oh yeah, and you love each other.

If he's cheating on his live-in girlfriend, it's basically the same as cheating on a wife. It doesn't speak well for his ethics, and it doesn't say much for how he would treat you if you ever got serious.

Did he move out when he started seeing you?

Yes. *Turn to page 92.*
No. *Turn to page 140.*

The Loner

Sometimes the people who say they like to be alone end up being the clingiest of all. When they find someone who can break through their solitude, the attachment becomes almost addictive. Turns out, they realize, companionship can be fun.

Does he want to spend *all* his time with you?

Yes, he's pretty needy. *Turn to page 126.*
No, he likes me, but he doesn't need to be together all the time. *Turn to page 164.*

Does he use his work as a reason to not see you very much?

Yes, he says he works too much. *Turn to page 82.*

No, he hasn't specifically mentioned work as a reason. *Turn to page 93.*

Leave a Message

His lack of a cell phone probably means one of two things: (1) He doesn't feel like footing the extra bucks for the monthly phone charge, or (2) he's not interested in being "on call" all the time. In any case, as long as he's still seeing you on a regular basis, his cellular deficiency shouldn't matter.

Turn to page 34.

Do you go out of your way for him?

Yes. *Turn to page 108.*
No. *Turn to page 112.*

Is he affectionate with you in public?

Yes. *Turn to page 99.*
No. *Turn to page 113.*

QUIZ RESULT: The "I'm So Busy" Guy

Advice: Find a guy who doesn't live at the office.

You have two choices: Hang in there with Mr. "I can't talk right now," or look for a guy who isn't too busy for you. Guys whose jobs get in the way of everything else are missing out on the most important part of the modern-day work ethic: You work to live, not vice versa.

Plus, even if he does have his nine-to-fives all booked up, he should be able to spare a few six-to-elevens for you. Most likely, when he says, "I'm really busy right now," what he really means is, "I don't want to spend what little free time I have with you."

Don't feel bad. It's common—albeit clichéd and perverse—to want the guys who don't want you. Be strong. Try changing the formula a bit: Go for a guy who doesn't have to pencil you in.

The Girl Next Door

It's only natural. You see him every day, you share the same refrigerator, you've already had the pleasure of seeing him fresh out of the shower, toweled and bare-chested. Really, there's only so much platonic partial nudity a girl can handle before she starts to think about whether there's more to being room-mates than splitting the telephone bill.

But be careful. He just got out of a relationship, and, whether he knows it or not, he could be using you as a doorway out of loneliness. Your doorway is, after all, pretty close to his.

Is he lonely and upset now that his last relationship has ended?

Yes, he seems bummed when he talks about it. *Turn to page 187.*
No, it doesn't seem to bother him. *Turn to page 84.*

Has there been chemistry between the two of you for a long time?

Yes. *Turn to page 89.*

No, I always thought of him as a friend until now.
Turn to page 87.

84

How long have you been dating him?

Less than a month. *Turn to page 152.*
More than a month. *Turn to page 100.*

How often does his ex-girlfriend come up in your conversations with him?

Pretty frequently. *Turn to page 111.*

Not that often. *Turn to page 114.*

How long have you known each other?

More than a year. *Turn to page 88.*
Less than a year. *Turn to page 90.*

QUIZ RESULT: High-Risk, High-Reward Relationship

Advice: "The bigger the risk, the greater the reward."

This'll end up either as the perfect story to tell at the wedding or the perfect story to tell when you're trying to warn your friends of the dangers of relationships with a roommate.

You're in hazardous territory, and you know it. You're probably tired of hearing that you're crazy, that it'll never work, or that you should go find something a little easier, less risky.

But you know what? All relationships are risky. You've already taken the first step; you might as well keep going and see what happens. If you fail, at least you'll have the story.

Home Sweet Home

Clearly, his last relationship wasn't that important to him, and by the looks of it, things have been brewing between the two of you for a while. So why not go with it?

Turn to page 90.

QUIZ RESULT: Roommates Plus

Advice: Get a month-to-month lease.

There's nothing like wall-to-wall intimacy to test whether a relationship is going to work. After all, what better way to find out if your love is real than to share a bathroom and bicker over things like whose turn it is to vacuum?

What you've got is a budding relationship without the ability to take things slowly. There is something to be said for being roommates: You don't have to agonize over whether you're ready to spend the night together; you don't have to wonder if it's okay to leave your toothbrush in his bathroom; and you don't need to worry about whether someone else is sleeping in his bed after you leave.

Really, the worst thing about dating your roommate is that you may end up with a really awkward, messy breakup that leaves you minus a boyfriend *and* a place to live.

Here's a tip: Unless you're sure about this one, don't buy furniture together.

Have you met his friends?

Yes. *Turn to page 81.*
No. *Turn to page 85.*

QUIZ RESULT: An Uphill Battle

Advice: This is going to take work.

Relationships are a little like jobs. Many people don't leave them until they have another one to go to. This is mainly because the alternative—simply leaving because they're not happy—is too risky, especially for those who can't stand being alone.

The fact that he doesn't mind jumping into a relationship with you doesn't mean his past is going to disappear. If it does, he's either not making deep connections or he has no trouble tossing his past feelings aside.

The fact that he's got some baggage doesn't mean your relationship is doomed, but it does mean that it's built on unstable ground. Should things get a little shaky, it could all come toppling down.

You knew this was complicated from the beginning. Most things that start out complicated only get more complicated. Tough it out, and maybe you'll get through without major damage.

Do you call him more than he calls you?

Yes. *Turn to page 94.*
No. *Turn to page 97.*

QUIZ RESULT: It's Not Going to Work

Advice: Find something that will.

Do you ever get the feeling that he's not completely there for you? Maybe he doesn't always call you back as quickly as he did when you first started dating. Maybe he *never* calls you back. Or maybe he calls but doesn't seem all that eager to take you out.

You probably knew from the beginning that this wasn't working, but for whatever reason you hung on, hoping that tomorrow or the next day he'd come around.

Reality check: He won't. While people can change, they often don't, or at least not until they've gotten to that point in their own time.

You're not alone. Most women have had at least one love affair with an impossible guy. In fact, the more impossible the man, the more attractive he appears. There are guys out there who will actually *want* to be with you. Go find them.

Penciling You In

It appears that, despite his heavy workload, he's still making the time to see you once a week. That's not bad.

Of course, true love is usually more than a once-a-week thing. But he does work a lot, so maybe he can't squeeze traditional love into his schedule right now. There's always later.

Turn to page 96.

Have you seen his workplace?

Yes. *Turn to page 190.*
No. *Turn to page 192.*

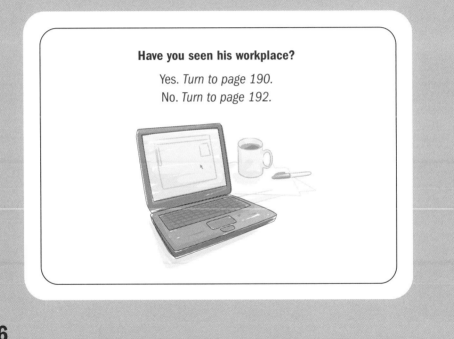

Making Time

Well, at least he's making an effort. But if your relationship is limited to every-so-often e-mails and phone chats, then you may as well be a client. Even the busiest of men still have to eat, sleep, and maybe have a beer. He could be doing these things with you. But is he?

How often do you go out with him?

Once a week. *Turn to page 95.*
Once every few weeks. *Turn to page 82.*
Once a month (or less). *Turn to page 94.*

Let's get this out of the way, then:

Do they have children together?

Yes. *Turn to page 109.*
No. *Turn to page 101.*

QUIZ RESULT: Could It Be Love?

Advice: Appreciate what you've got.

When you think about the fact that most relationships end pretty badly, you should feel pretty good about what you've got going with this guy right now. You're friends, you're attracted to each other, you can hold a conversation for more than five minutes. You may even feel a few butterflies in your stomach.

Yep. You're in love. And from the looks of it, he is too.

If you ever hear pesky voices in your head telling you that it's not going to work, that it's too good to be true, that any day now the other shoe's going to drop— ignore them. It *is* working, it *is* good, and there's no other shoe to be found.

You and he are destined for that elusive "next level," whatever that might mean to the two of you. Try to enjoy whatever level you're on now. You've got plenty of time to move up.

Where Are His Friends?

You've been going out with this guy for more than a month and you still haven't met any of his friends? Either he's the most unpopular guy on the block, or he's keeping you to himself because he doesn't plan on keeping you long.

Turn to page 67.

Playing with Fire

Unfortunately for you, he and his old flame have a history, and you're just the new girl. It's hard to walk the bridge from dating to friends without falling off a few times. Unless he's got a switch inside him that can turn off his feelings for her, she will probably complicate things.

Does he see her *more* than he sees you?

Yes. *Turn to page 111.*
No. *Turn to page 191.*

Visiting Hours

Many guys like to keep their workplace separate from their dating life. A guy may make an exception if his new girl is either really hot (she makes him look good in front of his officemates) or a "keeper" (he wants to include her in his life).

These rules don't hold true, however, if his workplace is open to the public. If he's a bartender and he's invited you to stop in for a drink on the house, that's not such a biggie. But if he's an accountant with a floor full of coworkers who'll see you enter and exit (and are likely to ask, "Who's that?"), that's a bit more meaningful.

Is his workplace open to the public?

No, he works in an environment that's off-limits to the public. *Turn to page 110.*
Yes, his workplace is open to the public. *Turn to page 185.*

Are You Appreciated?

Most men have been taught some basic manners and will give thanks where thanks are due. But there's more to appreciation than a simple thank you. If he's happy to be with you, he's going to show it.

Compliments are a low-cost, minimal-effort, highly effective way to achieve that.

Does he compliment you?

Yes. *Turn to page 67.*
No. *Turn to page 94.*

Is your relationship mostly physical?

Yes. *Turn to page 52.*
No, we're friends as well. *Turn to page 54.*

Is he on good terms with his ex-girlfriend?

Yeah, they're still friends. *Turn to page 107.*

No, they don't seem to like each other much.
Turn to page 106.

The Past Tells All

You can learn a lot about a guy by looking at his past relationships. It's kind of like buying a used car—you've got to know the history before driving it off the lot. But you can't learn much about his past unless he chooses to disclose it.

Do you know why he broke up with his ex?

Yes. He's told me about it. *Turn to page 135.*
Not really. He hasn't told me. *Turn to page 170.*

Do he and his ex still hang out a lot?

Yes. Sometimes I wonder . . . *Turn to page 98.*

No. They're friends, but they don't really see each other much. *Turn to page 191.*

Spoiling Him

This sounds more like a massage than a relationship: You're making all the effort, and he's just sitting back and enjoying it.

Turn to page 103.

Hanging with the Kiddies

Organizing weekend visits and explaining to his kids why you're sleeping in Daddy's bed isn't the ideal setting for a budding relationship. He's probably going through some things that will require a lot of patience on your part. And it's not going to be easy.

If you want to be with this guy, you're going to have to learn how to share.

Turn to page 92.

QUIZ RESULT: Slow-Motion Dating

Advice: It's gonna be a long way to the finish line.

He waits until the weekend to ask you out. He waits until you've gone out for at least half a year before he calls you his girlfriend. What you've got is a Slow-Motion Dater.

SMDs like to drag things out—either because they're not sure about the relationship, they're too busy to try harder, or they just don't get swept away like some people do.

This guy likes you, but it doesn't mean he's going to quit his Tuesday night bowling league or spend three nights in a row with you. This is the kind of relationship that, if it's going to work, is going to work slowly. And if you want it to work, you're going to have to be patient.

Think of it as a crossword puzzle: Things don't really get easy until you've done almost all the work. Then it just falls into place.

QUIZ RESULT: He's Not Moving On

Advice: You should.

You think that maybe if you were prettier, smarter, or funnier that then it would work? Or maybe if you were a better dancer, a better lover, a better friend, maybe then he'd love you?

But he won't. Really, the only way he'd love you is if you were his ex-girlfriend; she's the one he loves.

You can't really blame him. Sometimes it takes a while to get over a breakup. Sure, you may have seen glimpses of the person he'd be if he weren't so mired in heartache, but he's just not there yet.

Don't force him. Nothing you can do will snap him out of it. What you can do, however, is the one thing he can't: Find someone else.

Easy Street

At some level, all relationships require effort, and it doesn't look like either of you is putting any in. This is fine if you're not looking to get serious (not everyone is). But if you want something that's going to last, one of you is going to have to kick out of neutral and stop coasting. You won't get anywhere unless you put the car into drive.

Turn to page 67.

How does he introduce you to his friends?

As his girlfriend. *Turn to page 129.*
As his friend. *Turn to page 160.*
He just introduces me by name. *Turn to page 124.*

Stuck in the Middle

This guy sounds like he's teetering between swinging single and partnering up. Which he chooses probably depends on how much pressure you put on him. He knows that relationships can be great—he's been there. He also knows they can be a major pain.

Turn to page 120.

Facing the Truth

Calling what you've got a "relationship" would be like calling that stranger who bags your groceries your "best friend." It's not—and he's not. No matter how much you may *want* it to work between you and him, you're going to have to face the reality that it probably won't.

Turn to page 94.

In Denial

Sure, you can tell yourself he'll come around. You can tell yourself that maybe if you spend enough time with him, he'll realize how perfect the two of you are together. You can also tell yourself you're the queen of England.

When a guy says he's not ready for a relationship, what he really means is: He's not ready for a relationship. He doesn't say it to be cruel; he says it so you don't go on expecting more than he can give.

Turn to page 53.

How long have you been seeing him?

More than one month. *Turn to page 99.*
Less than one month. *Turn to page 57.*

QUIZ RESULT: A Higher Power

Advice: Have faith.

When a guy has enough faith to say no to sex, it's safe to say he's devoted. And the fact that you're equally devoted means you're on stable, equal footing. This guy is probably looking for a woman with similar values as himself, and from the looks of it, you might be that woman.

Bear in mind, however, that sharing the same religion does not a happy couple make. You might agree on some things, like whether you'll be reincarnated or are heaven-bound—but that doesn't mean your relationship will stand the test of time.

Religion aside, the most important things about a relationship are that you like being together and you work well as a couple. For now, enjoy the fact you've found someone with the same moral foundation, but don't substitute religious affinity for romantic love. You need both for this to work.

Tokens of Affection

If you casually mentioned your love of snow globes and the next day your guy showed up with a dozen of them, you'd be impressed, right? All materialism aside, thoughtful gifts can be a way of saying "I'm paying attention" without saying "I can't stop thinking about you."

Does he get you little gifts when there's no real occasion to do so?

Yes. *Turn to page 26.*
No. *Turn to page 145.*

Has he said any of the following things to you?

"I'm not ready to be in a relationship."

"I don't want a girlfriend."

"I don't want a commitment."

"You're too good for me."

"I've got a lot going on right now."

"I'm going through some things."

"I'm not ready to be exclusive."

Yes. *Turn to page 116.*
No. *Turn to page 123.*

120

When you are out together, do you and he ever share
"meaningful looks" from across the room?
(If this needs to be explained, then your answer is no.)

Yes. *Turn to page 99.*
No. *Turn to page 53.*

Taking His Time

This guy seems to be taking things really slowly. He calls once a week to set up your weekly dates, and you're lucky if he holds your hand at the movies.

Are you attracted to each other?

Yes. *Turn to page 110.*
No. *Turn to page 39.*

Is he affectionate with you when you're out together?

Yes, he's always rubbing my shoulders, tickling my back, or running his hands through my hair. *Turn to page 132.*

He holds my hand, but that's about it. *Turn to page 127.*

No, he's not very touchy-feely when we're out. *Turn to page 131.*

QUIZ RESULT: Limited Engagement

Advice: It's good for now, but don't expect a ring.

You can make believe this is going to last. But eventually, you're going to have to face the facts: This is not going to work.

It's working for now, you might say. But so is the Social Security Administration, and really, how long is that going to last?

What you've got is the relationship equivalent of a chocolate fudge sundae. It tastes great, but you know it's bad for you in the long run. And just as the occasional ice cream splurge can help improve your state of mind, the occasional short-lived relationship can help improve your self-esteem. If that's the case, gobble it up for now, but realize there's something better around the corner.

Does he have a lot of friends?

No, it doesn't seem like it. *Turn to page 77.*
Yes, I just haven't met them. *Turn to page 85.*

Do you want to spend all your time with him?

Yes. *Turn to page 16.*
No. *Turn to page 124.*

Holding Hands

Holding hands is vastly underrated—it can communicate love, affection, and attraction. It can also be clichéd or inappropriate. Only you can tell the difference.

Still stumped? Let's take a look at some of his other clues.

Turn to page 122.

Reciprocity

You like talking to him. You like kissing him. (Or if you haven't yet kissed, you can't wait to!) The big question now is: Does he feel the same way?

Is he attracted to you?

It sure seems like it! *Turn to page 46.*

Sometimes. It depends on what we're doing. *Turn to page 69.*

No. I feel like I'm not attractive to him. *Turn to page 39.*

A Big Step

To a lot of men, saying the word "girlfriend" is almost as big a deal as having one. But he's said it to you, and that's something you should be happy about. There's only one thing to worry about now:

Do you want to be his girlfriend?

Yes. *Turn to page 99.*
No. *Turn to page 55.*

Variety Is the Spice of Life

You're already ahead of the game. Having variety in your relationship is almost as important as having a relationship in the first place. Without mixing it up a little, relationships can get stale. As tempting as it may become to spend every night at home with your guy and a new release from the video store, it's going to get boring after a while. But you seem to know that already.

Turn to page 154.

Behind Closed Doors

Well, not everyone is into PDA. But he should be into NPDA (non-public displays of affection).

Is he affectionate with you when you're alone together?

Yes. *Turn to page 113.*
No. *Turn to page 122.*

Is he affectionate with you around his friends?

Yes, he's always affectionate.
It doesn't matter who's there. *Turn to page 148.*

No, he seems a little embarrassed in front of his friends.
Turn to page 113.

Making a Choice

If he's only been going out with her for a few months, it's not like you're breaking up a marriage. But that doesn't make it right; you're still breaking up something, and what does that say about his scruples? But if you think he's really a good guy caught in a bad situation—it does happen—tell him you don't want to share, so he'll have to make a choice.

Turn to page 140.

QUIZ RESULT: The Cheater

Advice: Leave before you're on the receiving end.

No matter how many times they hear the old warning "Once a cheater, always a cheater," women will continue to fall for guys who are taken, clinging to the idea that this time that old saying won't apply. "Not with this guy," they think. "This is different."

That's nonsense. Now's your chance to have some self-respect and get away from this guy before the relationship, if that's what you want to call it, lands you on the therapist's couch wondering why you always go for guys you can't get.

Save yourself the 100 bucks an hour: The answer is that it's most likely the lure of the challenge. Maybe the prospect of attaining the unattainable boosts your self-esteem.

Here's what you have to remember: If this guy is as great as you think he is, he'd look you in the eyes and tell you, "Sorry, I can't," even if he wanted to.

Learning from the Past

Bravo on getting your guy to open up to you! Letting a current girlfriend in on what went wrong with the last one takes courage on his part. Either he's interested in you and wants you to know all his complications or he's indirectly trying to say he's not over his breakup yet.

What were their problems?

Mostly small stuff—differences in opinion and petty arguments. *Turn to page 136.*

They had some serious issues. *Turn to page 171.*

The Little Things

It's not the mountainous issues that divide us; it's the little things—the differences of opinion, the pesky habits.

Many couples break up because of the small stuff. Maybe she hated the way he parted his hair; maybe he hated the way she color-coded her closet. Even if you have a great sex life and "look cute together," you need a solid foundation of common goals and interests to keep those little annoyances from ruining what you've got. Do you have the "more than" to make it?

Turn to page 169.

Being the Other Woman

Unfortunate though this situation may be, it's very common. A lot of relationships end because one person meets someone else.

A good guy, however, will get out of the current one as quickly as possible to avoid hurting his girlfriend (and being an all-out jerk) by continuing a relationship behind her back. If you've been seeing him for a while and he's juggling the two of you with a mere promise of changing things "soon," he may not be worth the fight.

How long have you been dating him?

Less than a month. *Turn to page 138.*
More than a month. *Turn to page 134.*

Are you sleeping together?

Yes. *Turn to page 134.*
No. *Turn to page 92.*

Is this a long-distance relationship?

Yes. *Turn to page 43.*
No. *Turn to page 74.*

Does he plan on ending things with her?

Yes, he says he will. *Turn to page 141.*

Eventually. *Turn to page 137.*

We haven't talked about it. *Turn to page 134.*

Do you believe him?

Yes. *Turn to page 92.*
No. *Turn to page 134.*

Oh, so it's one of *those* relationships. You're dating him, but you don't want to let him get too close.

Why is that?

Because I don't think it'll last. *Turn to page 124.*
Because we're taking things slow. *Turn to page 110.*
I'm just not that into him. *Turn to page 39.*

Not a Good Sign

You can tell yourself "He's probably busy" when you've already called him three times just to get a rushed "Can I call you back?" While you're at it, you can tell yourself he lost your number, he lost his cell phone, or, better yet, "He's just shy."

Maybe he is busy, but if he were interested, he'd spend his few spare moments of potential phone time calling you.

Turn to page 94.

Meeting the Boys

Not all guys can be insta-boyfriends. It sounds as if he's trying, though.

A guy usually brings a girl around for one of two reasons: either to show her off or to get his friends' approval. If she passes the test, the friends generally start giving her subtle cues, like saying, "Take care of our boy."

In fact, sometimes the best way to find out if a guy likes you is to see how his friends act around you. If he's been complaining to them about the way you follow him around like a puppy (even if you don't), it's not likely they're going to buddy up with you the moment you walk in the room. If he's been talking you up, however, they're probably going to make some effort to make you feel like you belong.

Do his friends act as if you're his girlfriend?

Yes, they're all really nice to me. *Turn to page 121.*
Not really. Sometimes I don't think they even know we're dating. *Turn to page 113.*

Giving Other Things

Maybe he's not the gift-giving type; that doesn't necessarily mean he's not into you. The question really should be: Has he given himself to you. (And before your dirty little mind gets any further into the gutter, we're talking emotionally.)

Will he talk about who he is? Does he tell you when he's worried about his job or his friends? Can he share how he feels about intimate issues like love, religion, and whether it's fair that the Yankees dominate the world of baseball?

In other words, do you think he's opened up emotionally to you?

Yes. *Turn to page 21.*
No. *Turn to page 92.*

**Does his religion require him
to stay celibate until marriage?**

Yes. *Turn to page 147.*
No. *Turn to page 44.*

Conflicts of Interest

So he's waiting until marriage to have sex—that's devotion. If you're not as devout, you can bet you two are going to have a lot more to worry about than whether it's OK to kiss on the first date.

Do you share the same religious beliefs?

Yes. *Turn to page 118.*
No. *Turn to page 48.*

This One's a Keeper

This guy's not playing any games. He likes you, and he's not afraid to show it—even in front of the boys. If you're worried about this relationship, you're crazy. It seems like you've got a good one.

Turn to page 35.

Benefit of the Doubt

For the sake of optimism, let's assume he really is too busy to go out much. Still, if he really liked you, he'd be making the effort to find some time to see you, even if it was just once or twice a month.

Does he call you and ask you out?

Yes, he's the one calling me. *Turn to page 151.*
No, I am usually the one initiating our dates. *Turn to page 150.*

Swimming Solo

If you're the one always calling him, and he's only willing to give up a small slice of his time, it's not likely that he's in passionate, desperate love with you. Even if those two dates a month are the most spectacular hours of your life, they might not be all that special to him. Is he having fun? Maybe. Are you important to him? Don't bet on it.

Sometimes getting a relationship to work is all about catching a guy at the right time. Your timing could have been a little off on this one.

Turn to page 94.

Does he have a very demanding job?

Yes. *Turn to page 82.*
No. *Turn to page 143.*

On Schedule

You may be spending a good amount of time with this guy, but obviously nothing's serious yet. And how could it be, really? You're still new to each other. An important thing to assess at this early stage is his reliability. Does he call when he says he will? On "the morning after," if he promises to call you later, it *should* mean he'll call you later that day. Not later that month.

Turn to page 177.

Time Well Spent?

It's great to spend a lot of time together, but there could be a problem if you only hang out on his couch. It's also not a good sign if you only get together when you both feel like hitting the town. Ideally, there should be a balance.

Do you spend most of your time at home?

Yes. *Turn to page 104.*
No, we're usually out at restaurants, clubs, parties, etc. *Turn to page 81.*
It's about 50/50. *Turn to page 130.*

How are your conversations?

Great. We can talk for hours. *Turn to page 196.*

Okay, but I don't hang out with him
for the conversation. *Turn to page 104.*

How long have you been going out with him?

More than a month. *Turn to page 180.*

Less than a month. *Turn to page 181.*

We're not dating yet; we've just discussed the possibility.
Turn to page 189.

Instant Complications

Dating a practically married guy is trouble. The situation is near impossible if you're also dealing with children.

Does he have young kids living nearby?

Yes. *Turn to page 157.*
No. *Turn to page 161.*

Daddy Love

Wake up and smell the diapers! In the land of divorce papers and fatherhood, there's not much room for the spark of new love. If he tells you he loves you now, he could always plead temporary insanity later. And he wouldn't be lying.

Turn to page 92.

Class Clown

Contrary to what you might think, great looks might actually be a handicap for some guys, as they can be intimidating to many women. Women like a pretty face as much as men do, but most women will give an average-looking guy a chance if he's got brains, confidence, success, and a sense of humor.

The fact that your guy's not Adonis shouldn't really have prevented him from finding a girlfriend. Maybe he's got intimacy or commitment issues? Maybe he can't get serious.

Does he always seem like he's "keeping things light"?

Yes, he's always joking around, and he doesn't talk about his feelings much. *Turn to page 159.*

No, he seems comfortable talking about anything and has already told me a lot of personal things about his past. *Turn to page 154.*

Do you feel like you can open up to him?

Yes, I feel like I can tell him anything.
Turn to page 67.

No, I feel uncomfortable talking about some things.
Turn to page 94.

Afraid to Say It?

It's fine if he's introducing you as a friend because you've only gone on three dates and he's just not sure what to call you yet. But if you've been going out—and making out—for a while now, he should recognize that you're more than just a "friend."

How long have you been dating?

Less than two months. *Turn to page 152.*
More than two months. *Turn to page 124.*

Things Could Be Better

Well, it's not the best of beginnings, but stranger things have happened. You've got to treat this relationship very carefully. If he says he needs space, don't sweat it, and give it to him.

Turn to page 198.

Rebounding

Sure, it's possible he was deeply in love with his ex, but the likelihood would be greater if he'd been with her for, say, five or ten years. That would be baggage. Less than a year? That's a tote bag.

So let's look at the two of you. Besides attraction, conversation is a pretty important part of a relationship. It'd get pretty boring after a while just gazing and cuddling your way through every weekend.

Do you and he have a lot to talk about?

Yeah, we talk all the time. *Turn to page 120.*

We're not in constant conversation, but we can talk to each other.
Turn to page 21.

Not really. Sometimes the conversation seems forced. *Turn to page 163.*

Forcing the Issue

Forcing conversation out of some guys is like squeezing the last glob of toothpaste out of the tube. It takes a lot of twisting and prodding.

There's nothing wrong with a casual fling now and then. But if the relationship is taking more effort than it's worth, you're going to have to face the facts and end it.

Why do you like him?

I think he's interesting. *Turn to page 173.*

He's cute. *Turn to page 175.*

I don't like him all that much, but I've got nothing else going on right now. *Turn to page 67.*

In a Good Space

Whoever made up that "I can't live without you" mumbo-jumbo was obviously not in a healthy relationship. Independence is a good thing. Without it, we'd all still be living at home with our parents.

You should be thankful that your guy doesn't need to spend every waking minute with you. You want a boyfriend, not a shadow.

Turn to page 168.

Potential for "Underload"

There's overload and there's *underload*. While dating a guy who's stuck to you can cramp your style, seeing him less often than you pay your rent is definitely not a good sign.

Turn to page 197.

Does he work a lot?

Yes, his job takes up all his time. *Turn to page 78.*
No, his job is no more demanding than most.
Turn to page 143.

Do you think he's a good kisser?

Yeah, he's great! *Turn to page 124.*
He's nothing to brag about. *Turn to page 67.*
Honestly, he's awful. *Turn to page 45.*
I haven't kissed him yet. *Turn to page 172.*

Full Disclosure

The fact that you're spending some time as two separate people (a good thing) instead of becoming one big relationship blob doesn't mean he should go MIA every time you're not looking.

A guy who's trying to let a girl into his life will tell her what he's up to when she's not around. For example, did he tell you all about hanging with the guys last Saturday night, or is he evasive when you bring up the subject?

Does he talk about what he's doing when he's not with you?

Yes, he always tells me what he's doing when we're not together. *Turn to page 35.*

No, he keeps that to himself. *Turn to page 53.*

Under the Microscope

Whether you mean to or not, being in a relationship means you'll end up noticing all those little things about your partner that the casual acquaintance won't always see. You'll find yourself focusing on the little things—the way he says your name, the way he shuts his door, the way he chews his food.

In the end, anything that *could* bother you probably will. Consequently, you'd better make sure you're prepared.

Does he have any characteristics (in his appearance or mannerisms) that bother you?

Yes, but it's no big deal. *Turn to page 179.*
Not that I've seen yet! *Turn to page 34.*

Mysterious Past

Women settle their relationship woes by gathering together with friends and communally dissecting The Boyfriend's every move. Men don't often dwell too much on unhappy topics. He probably doesn't want to talk about his last girlfriend because he doesn't want to put himself in a bad mood.

Let's not dwell on this—let's find out about you two.

Turn to page 8.

How long were they going out?

More than a year. *Turn to page 92.*
Less than a year. *Turn to page 162.*

Why not?

He says he's "not ready" to get involved yet. *Turn to page 111.*

I'm not attracted to him. *Turn to page 45.*

I don't know—he just hasn't tried yet. *Turn to page 176.*

Sugar Daddy

You describe him as "interesting" even though you don't have much to talk about. Let's take a guess: Is he a doctor? A hotel heir? A rock star, maybe?

You already said your conversations are a bit lacking—what's so "interesting" about that? Most likely, the person you like is some fantasy version of this guy, not the actual guy sitting in front of you with his lips stitched together.

Does his salary or prestige have anything to do with why you like him?

It's irrelevant. I'd like him even if he were a chimney sweep. *Turn to page 174.*
Yes, I admire his line of work. *Turn to page 124.*

What keeps him coming back to you?

The chemistry. We can't keep our hands off each other!
Turn to page 52.

Well, he's not really "coming back" to me yet.
I don't see him very often. *Turn to page 124.*

We like to do the same sorts of things. *Turn to page 167.*

Trophy Boy

It's fine to mingle with the beautiful people if the beautiful people don't make you feel like a second-class citizen. If your guy is treating you well, then let him be your accessory for a while. But if he's a jerk, then it's not worth the trouble, no matter how great he looks in a tux.

Does he call you when he says he will?

Every time! He's very reliable. *Turn to page 67.*
Not always. He sometimes "forgets" to call me. *Turn to page 61.*

How many times have you gone out with him?

Three or more times. *Turn to page 45.*
Fewer than three times. *Turn to page 178.*

Does he call you when he says he will?

Yes. If he says "I'll call you tomorrow," I know it's true.
Turn to page 110.

No. Sometimes he says he'll call, but then I won't hear
from him for a few days. *Turn to page 66.*

Last Words

You've either scored the last remaining gentleman on the planet, or your guy's giving you mixed signals for a reason. Maybe he doesn't like you in "that way." Maybe he's interested in someone else. Maybe he thinks you don't like him.

How can you tell? Usually, if a guy's interested in a girl as more than a friend, he'll end a date with something a little more than "Race you to the bus stop!"

How does he end your dates?

He gives me a kiss on the cheek and tells me he'll call me tomorrow. *Turn to page 110.*

He says "See ya!" and drives away. *Turn to page 45.*

From Better to Worse

You can handle his little flaws now, sure. But what about a year or two down the road, when you've heard one too many post-soda belches and grown tired of his blonde jokes?

The beginning of a relationship is supposed to be the magic time, when flaws are invisible, when love is blind, when all the things that will someday make you crazy seem perfectly adorable. If you're already finding fault with this guy, it's not going to get any better.

Turn to page 124.

No-Win Situation

There's just no way to look at this situation positively. Any guy with a shred of decency would end things with his wife before letting a new relationship reach the one-month mark. Don't try to rationalize it; don't give him any excuses. No matter what problems he's having at home, none of them are as serious as the problems he's created by being with you.

Turn to page 47.

Trusting a Cheater

Maybe you have visions of happily ever after with this guy, once he moves out of his wife's house, gets his divorce papers signed, and navigates his way through the inevitable mountain of emotional baggage that he'll be toting once his marriage officially dissolves.

But is that really what you want? Establishing trust in a relationship born of an affair is like choosing a housesitter from a kleptomania support group.

Turn to page 134.

Paying Attention

Unless it's God calling with some commandments to be carried out pronto, most guys won't even consider answering the phone when they're in the middle of an important date. Which leads to the next question: How important is this date?

There may be other things he's doing to clue you in to his feelings (or lack of them) for you. For one thing, eye contact. If his eyes glaze over like those of a 12-year-old in geography class when you try to communicate with him, he's probably not interested.

Does he pay attention to you when you're talking?

Yes. He asks me lots of questions and seems interested in what I have to say. *Turn to page 186.*

No, he does most of the talking. *Turn to page 53.*

We don't really talk much. *Turn to page 184.*

Job with Benefits

Working with a guy you're dating *should* open up all sorts of opportunities for seeing him more than just once a week. You should be having after-work cocktails, after-work dinners, and end-of-the-day in-the-conference-room makeout sessions.

So why are you only seeing this guy once a week?

Turn to page 67.

If you're not talking much, what *are* you doing?

Making out, mostly. We're really attracted to each other.
Turn to page 52.

We just do things that don't really require talking,
like going to the movies and seeing concerts. *Turn to page 67.*

Stopping By

The good news: He's not ashamed of you. (Otherwise he wouldn't want you to be seen by his coworkers.)

The bad news: He's probably invited lots of other people to visit him at work, too. Guys who work in public places—stores, bars, restaurants, etc.—generally make a habit of telling people to "stop by." Still, the fact he asked you says *something*.

Turn to page 120.

Split Personality

You probably don't know exactly where you stand with this guy, and there's a good reason for that. It sounds like you're dealing with someone who doesn't know what he wants. Sometimes it's you; sometimes it's the pasta with garlic sauce. When he's not giving you his full attention, he's not giving you much attention at all.

Turn to page 124.

Knocking at Your Door

You've always been "just friends," but now that suddenly he's wallowing in post-breakup depression, it occurred to him that you could be more than that. After all, he's lonely, and you're *another woman*.

Whether it's a good idea or not, guys aren't always discriminating when choosing their rebounds. He's chosen you, but be careful. It's hard enough to start a new relationship; it's even harder when you're going to see each other every morning.

Turn to page 87.

Does he live very far from you?

Yes, he's at least a few hours away. *Turn to page 71.*
No. He lives nearby. *Turn to page 149.*

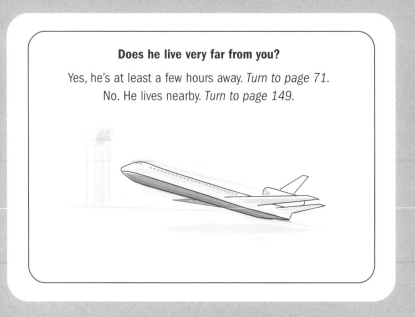

How long has he been married?

Less than a year. *Turn to page 134.*
Between one and five years. *Turn to page 92.*
More than five years. *Turn to page 47.*

Do you work together?

Yes. *Turn to page 183.*
No. *Turn to page 102.*

Friendly Terms

If he's spending the once-in-a-blue-moon lunch date with his ex, it only means he's a nice enough guy that she doesn't hate his guts post-breakup. This is a good thing. He can have female friends; it means he's not a jerk.

As long as he's not returning from said visitations a little tipsy and smelling faintly of perfume, you have nothing to worry about. She was a part of his life, after all. It's a good thing he's not so eager to dump his past.

So let's move on to the two of you.

Turn to page 8.

Visitation Rights

Don't feel bad. Unless his office has a "Bring Your Girlfriend to Work" day, most workplaces just aren't conducive to visitors. And really, unless he's the hottest male stripper in town (and that adds a whole new set of complications), what more could you learn by seeing him in the throes of professionalism?

If you're dating a guy who's also dating his job, it's important that he tell you a little about it, just so you understand what all the fuss is about and why, at the end of the day, he's stressed more often than not. This doesn't mean he should give you every detail, but he shouldn't get all tight-lipped when you ask him politely, "How was your day?"

Does he talk about his job with you?

Yes, all the time. *Turn to page 110.*

Not really; he doesn't seem to think it's important. *Turn to page 124.*

I haven't asked him about work, but I'm sure he'd talk about it if I did. *Turn to page 193.*

Are you interested in what he has to say?

Not really. Our relationship is more physical than conversational.
Turn to page 52.

Yes, but talking about work is boring. *Turn to page 124.*

Once a week is fine in the very beginning, but after a few dates you should be building up more momentum.

How many times have you gone out with him?

Once or twice. *Turn to page 177.*
Three or four times. *Turn to page 114.*
More than four times. *Turn to page 195.*

Does his job prevent you from seeing him more?

Yes, he's got a really demanding job. *Turn to page 82.*
No, I don't think that's the problem. *Turn to page 124.*

One Last Thing

Things seem pretty near perfect. There's just one more thing: You need to make sure you've got that butterflies-in-the-stomach feeling.

Are you attracted to each other?

Yes, we're all over each other! *Turn to page 99.*
Not really. The chemistry's not there. *Turn to page 39.*

Office Flirt

The daily grind is a lot more tolerable when you spend it chatting over e-mail and engaging in casual walk-by conversations. He's probably had ample opportunity to slip in the occasional flirtation; if not, your "dates" with this guy aren't going to get very far very fast.

Does he flirt with you at work or school?

Yes, he's always e-mailing me, and he talks to me whenever he's close by. *Turn to page 110.*

No, we don't really talk much at work/school. *Turn to page 94.*

Do you spend a lot of time with him?

Yes, we're together all the time. *Turn to page 153.*

I see him about once a week. *Turn to page 8.*

No, I only see him once a month or so. *Turn to page 188.*